Good manners
cultivated in childhood
can make us happy
and successful in life.
1901

"Have you seen the jewels, Lady Curwen?"
Tom asked presently.

# ETIQUETTE
# FOR THE
# CHILDREN

Copper Beech Publishing

Published in Great Britain by
Copper Beech Publishing Ltd
© Copper Beech Publishing 2001

ISBN
978 1 898617 29 7
1 898617 29 5

A CIP catalogue record for this book is available from
The British Library

Edited by Julie Hinton

Copper Beech Publishing Ltd
P O Box 159  East Grinstead
Sussex  England RH19 4FS

# Including

A proper training
Set a good example
Early childhood
Dress
Good manners in person
Good habits
At the table
In general life
Respect for superiors
Entering a room
Parties for children
Notes for grown girls
Using persuasion
A word of encouragement
Morals
Governess
Pocket-money
Speech
Self-consciousness
Kindness
A word to parents
A word to teachers
Moral maxims

## A HELPFUL GUIDE

This little book is meant to be a helpful guide for little children and their parents.

Politeness seems to be born with boys and girls, yet, through neglect and carelessness, the children sometimes form bad habits that destroy their natural courtesy and charm of manner.

In every house where there are children, a great responsibility rests upon the parents.

To provide proper food and suitable clothing, and to do all possible to ensure the health of the children, is but a part of the duty of parents. Much more remains to be done.

To train and educate the children both mentally and physically is another portion of the task imposed upon them and to successfully carry out the undertaking entails much thought and consideration on the part of fathers, mothers, or guardians of the young people.

## A HELPFUL GUIDE

Parents, teachers and children who read this little book should take take no offence where none is meant. Seeing these few notes in print will do more to cure bad habits in the little ones than constant correction.

Now that so many advantages are given by a liberal education, innate courtesy and warmness of heart will be fully developed and good manners will be the result.

A great deal of a person's success in life depends upon the training he has received during infancy and childhood.                              1901

## A PROPER TRAINING

**P**arents, teach your children obedience first
- that is the mainspring upon which all other virtues
move. Honesty, industry, affection, thrift, manliness,
womanliness, and indeed everything which is necessary to the formation of a good man or woman will
take root in the heart and bear fruit later in life of those
who have been properly trained in infancy.

Adversity may overtake them, sickness may weaken
them, a cold world may frown on them, but amidst
all let memory carry them back to a home where the
love of kindness reigned - where the mother's re-
proving eye was moistened with a tear, and the father
frowned 'more in sorrow than in anger'.

## SET A GOOD EXAMPLE

**A good example** should be set by parents to their children upon all occasions, both in their powers of self-control and their courtesy of demeanour towards each other.

Never give way to temper before a child nor enter into quarrelling or argument of any kind.

It must be remembered that in little ones the imitative faculties are developed to an almost abnormal extent, and that a child's character will receive lasting impressions from those with whom he comes into contact in early childhood.

Let an effort be made, therefore, that he shall never learn anything but good from his surroundings.

## EARLY CHILDHOOD

**G**ood **manners should be cultivated** from earliest childhood, as they will always be the means of making us happy and successful in life. Good manners should be as carefully observed at home as abroad.

No person can be really good mannered without being kind hearted and unselfish and no home is happy where those in it do not practise these virtues.

## DRESS

**To be clean and tidy in our dress** is the first proof of good manners, showing respect to those we mix with. A dirty and untidy child is an insult to those she meets. Expense is not necessary for neat dressing; care of clothes is the great point.

Clothes should be mended immediately when torn, they should be washed when soiled, but they *never* should be worn either torn or soiled.

A child who is not old enough to mend or wash for herself can get it done for her, but from the age of seven years a child ought to be taught to mend and wash. Buttons should never be left wanting; and above all, pins should not be put in their place, it is a dangerous and very slovenly habit.

*Have a scrupulous regard to neatness of person.
Broken strings and tangled hair are signs that little
girls are not very industrious or regular
in their habits.*

## *Advice for good manners*

Nowadays it seems to be the fashion for mothers
to take their children about with them every-
where. Dressed like little fashion plates, they are
taken to pay calls, to At Homes, to luncheons and
dinners at restaurants – they are, in fact, treated
as little men and women of the world and
encouraged to show off upon all occasions.
To every right-feeling mother there can be no
more sorry spectacle than that presented by an
over-dressed precocious child laying herself out for
admiration and attention and conducting herself
with all the savoir faire of a woman of thirty!
The child is thus robbed of the best joys of
childhood by turning her into a little woman
before her time!

## GOOD MANNERS IN PERSON

**B**esides being neat and tidy in dress, our persons must be clean - face, neck, ears, hands, arms, teeth, nails - and little girls, particularly, should take great pride in such matters. The hair should be washed and the whole person should be frequently washed by taking a bath.

## GOOD HABITS

**B**esides good manners in dress, good manners must also be observed in our habits. Always use a pocket handkerchief, never use the apron, or, worse still, a habit which should hardly be mentioned - the fingers.

Pocket handkerchiefs can be had for 1d. and last - with care - a long time, but they must be washed always, when soiled. Never use the handkerchief for wiping slates, a sponge or rag should always be kept for the purpose.

Avoid when possible using the handkerchief too much in public, or at table, but when suffering from a cold, this is unavoidable. Avoid coughing loudly; never snuffle (a rude ugly noise with the nose) - and be as particular about these matters by oneself as in public.

## *Advice for good manners*

We owe as much to ourselves as to others.
Never put out the tongue; never bite the nails or
clean them in public.
Never scratch the head and avoid all other repul-
sive habits.
Never spit on the floor or about a room; spitting
is unnecessary at any time, it is a coarse
and ugly habit.
Never spit on knives and forks to clean them, or
into the bathbrick when making it into paste;
always use cold water.
There is no cleaning virtue in spittle, though some
ignorant people give this as an excuse.

## *Advice for good manners*

The children should be as much as possible with people of refinement. During the years which intervene between babyhood and the age at which lessons may begin, it is a good plan to engage a lady to be with the little ones for a few hours daily, taking them for their walks, and making their deportment and manners her special care. For the mother who has a number of social duties which preclude her from spending as much time with her children as she would wish, such a plan has much in its favour.

## AT THE TABLE

❧

**It is above all at the table**, when eating meals, that good manners should be observed from infancy.

No child, even of two years of age, should be permitted to be rude or vulgar. In eating, always eat with the lips closed; do not eat so that the food can be seen in the mouth, and never drink when food is in the mouth; finish what you are eating and then take a drink.

### Noise

Never make any noise when drinking, and never put too much food at a time into the mouth.

### Bread

Cut bread small and butter it; do not put a slice into the mouth and drag away what is not eaten. Never put the knife into the mouth, even with cheese; it is very dangerous and quite incorrect.

### Elbows

Sit up straight; keep the elbows well in, never put the elbows on the table.

### Knives and forks

Hold the knives and forks by the handles only, never by the blade or prongs; keep the knives and forks well down, never turned up, resting the elbows on the table.

### Always ask

Never stretch across the table for food, always ask for what is required, and take care to look round and see that those near you have all that they require.

### Never use the tablecloth

When finished eating, draw the knife and fork together on the plate. Never wipe the mouth with the table cloth, use a table napkin or the pocket handkerchief.

### Greedy

Do not sit down and think only of yourself, eating away as fast as possible, as greedy little girls and boys sometimes do. Give others the best of everything, never pick the best for yourself, it is rude and very selfish, and no child should help herself before those older than her.

### *The habit of conversation*

Little ones should give themselves the habit of carrying on a pleasant conversation at the table, but all disagreeable or low and vulgar subjects should be avoided.

### *Cleanliness*

They should always be clean and neat, but above all at the table, a soiled face and soiled hands is unpardonable, and a child should be sent away from the table if she dares to appear unprepared.

### *Dipping bread into the gravy*

Some children have the habit of dipping bread into the gravy on the dish, this must not be allowed.

### *Pudding*

When eating pudding the fingers should never be used to push the pudding on to the spoon, a little piece of crust should be used if children are too young to use a fork.

### Begin well

At breakfast, in the morning, a child should appear as clean as at dinner; some little boys and girls tumble out of bed, rush down to breakfast, and never think of washing and tidying themselves. This is an insult to those breakfasting with them, but it is a very bad habit easily cured.

Begin the day well, look clean and bright and tidy and remain so during the day; try it for a week and you will persevere for ever with a little courage.

### Tea and coffee

Never blow tea or coffee to cool it; add cold milk if necessary. Never put tea, coffee or milk into the saucer to cool, it is very vulgar to do so. If children see those older than themselves doing it they must on no account correct them as it would be very hurtful and wrong.

## *Advice for good manners*

In most families the children join their parents at luncheon, this being the dinner-hour for the little ones. This is a very good custom, as it enables them to acquire the manners and deportment to be observed at table.

A mother should begin early to train her child in this direction. Properly trained children can be allowed to sit at the luncheon table when friends are present, without any qualms of anxiety being felt by the parents as to how they will behave, whilst ill-mannered children will be a source, not only of shame to the parents, but annoyance to their guests.

### Butter

When taking butter use a separate knife. Generally a butter knife is laid beside the butter; never use your own knife.

### Eat slowly

Never eat too quickly, it is very rude and very bad for the health; eat slowly with lips closed and chew all food well.

### Sucking the teeth

Never at meals suck the teeth making a peculiar smack, it is a very bad habit, though very often met with.

### Fingers

Never use the fingers with food and never take bones in the fingers to pick; cut the meat from them. Cut potatoes in four and remove the peel with both knife and fork.

### A rude and greedy habit

Never put food such as fruit cake, etc. from the table into the pocket. It is a very rude and greedy habit and would give people the idea that the children never had enough to eat.

### Grace

Always say grace before and after meals.

### Speaking

Avoid speaking with any food in the mouth, finish what you are eating and then speak. Ask very politely for anything you require, saying 'Will you kindly pass me the salt' or 'May I trouble you for the salt' – and say 'thank you' when it is passed.

### Stones

If you meet stones in jam, etc. slip the stones from the mouth on to the spoon, or if the stones are in fruit such as plums or cherries, slip the stone through the fingers on to the plate.

### Using a teaspoon

When drinking tea never leave the spoon in the cup, and when stirring tea do not stir it roughly as if you wanted to take the bottom out of the cup. Stir tea gently.

## GOOD MANNERS IN GENERAL LIFE

ᘒᕷ

**Little boys** should show deference to little girls, opening the door for them, removing their hats while doing so, if they are wearing hats.

Little boys when walking with little girls, should walk on the outside of the path, and from their earliest days should be taught to lift their hats when the little girls bow, as there is no reason why little boys and girls should not begin to be polite from early childhood.

Little girls should open the door for their superiors and their elders, to show respect. To our superiors we should show not only politeness, but great respect, stand up when addressed by them, and remain standing until told to sit down.

Offer to carry parcels, saying 'Kindly permit me' and if refused, do not insist.

## RESPECT FOR SUPERIORS

**Respect** to our superiors is the foundation of good manners.

When speaking to them use their titles and when answering never say Yes, No; say Yes Maam or No Maam, Yes Miss or No Miss.

Never be impertinent to superiors or give rude short answers such as when asked 'Why did you do so and so?' 'Because I liked it' - and so on. Such habits show great want of careful training and grow up with children, causing them to be greatly disliked.

All through life they will have someone in authority over them to respect, and if allowed to be disrespectful when children, when they grow up they will be unbearable.

When spoken to, a child should hold up her head, answer audibly and most respectfully; it is very bad manners to hang down the head and refuse to answer.

## ENTERING A ROOM

**Learn to enter a room** modestly, but without an air of shyness and fear. Speak frankly, and with a cordial grace to your mamma's friends, giving them your hand, or bowing slightly, but courteously if they are strangers.

The shyness of some poor children on entering a room is truly pitiable. They look absolutely cross and haughty from their own awkward fear of others; and are dumb from the effect of this same terrible *mauvais honte*.

At the same time, it would be very unbecoming in a little girl to talk much, or to interrupt a conversation, as some spoiled children will occasionally do.

## PARTIES FOR CHILDREN

෨෨

**T**he eldest girl can learn to act the part of hostess, receive her guests and learn a little unselfishness by making herself responsible for the comfort and happiness of her guests. A mother would do well to guide her young in the way a party should go.

Proper rooms should be provided for the young guests, with maids to assist them and they should be made to feel like young grown-up people.

*No trouble should be spared over the arrangement of the supper table which is laid out as it would be for the mother's own guests. Although of course no wine should be served!*

The young hostess should discuss matters with her wise mother and decide in advance what can and what cannot be done. All of this will be invaluable practice for years to come when she must be hostess at much more elaborate and extensive affairs.

## NOTES FOR GROWN GIRLS

෧෨

**P**resuming that little girls have grown up and are leaving school, the following notes may be useful to them.

A lady bows first to a gentleman, then he takes off his hat, not before. A gentleman, when walking with a lady, should walk on the outside of the street.

Going up stairs, a gentleman goes first; down stairs, a gentleman goes last.

A gentleman should always open a door for a lady and allow her to pass through.

Grown up girls, having left school, should at once insist on receiving the greatest respect from gentlemen. No familiarity should be allowed; there is an old saying 'Familiarity breeds contempt' – and it is very true. The more respect a girl commands the more she will receive, and the more highly she will be thought of even by those whom she may have found necessary to repulse in the first instance for familiarity.

Boys and girls, from earliest infancy, should be ladies and gentlemen, and parents should insist on boys showing deference to girls.

A boy of seven years or younger can easily be taught to raise his cap when a little girl bows, then in later life these habits become natural.

In a crush or crowd, men should protect women from danger. Only a cowardly man pushes through a crowd at the risk of hurting women.

## *Advice for good manners*

No one is perfect, and if our elders do make
mistakes it is because in their youth they had not
the advantages of children in the present day.
When one has grown old it is not easy to
change bad habits.

## USING PERSUASION

᠑

**H**ome is the child's first school, and, if the child is taught and trained properly therein by those whose duty it is to instruct the young mind, the boy or girl will assuredly grow up and become an honour and credit to parents and teachers. 'To train up a child in the way it should go' does not imply that 'if you spare the rod you spoil the child.'

Punishing a child for some slight fault on the plea that the punishment will deter it from doing wrong on a future occasion is *not* a satisfactory method. Yet how many parents there are who endeavour to train their children by this mode of procedure.

To train a child successfully can be often more readily done by persuasion than by resorting to severe measures.

## A WORD OF ENCOURAGEMENT

∾

**A mother should never permit** her child to get beyond bounds or control, otherwise it is very possible that it will take advantage of the latitude allowed to it.

A word of encouragement here and there is of the utmost value in helping a child to be good. Let not this encouragement be withheld, and be ready to reward the little ones for any special pains taken in overcoming some fault or performing some - to them - difficult task.

Discretion must also govern the form which the reward must take. Parents are too apt to give money or sweets indiscriminately on these occasions, encouraging involuntarily a love of extravagance and even greediness in their children.

Gifts of this kind now and then will do no harm, but do not let the reward always take this form.

*Advice for good manners*

Such treats as a walk or a picnic in the country,
or permission to invite some little friends to tea,
will be appreciated by children who are brought
up in a becomingly simple manner, and who will
hail with delight any little departure from the
ordinary routine.

*"One good mother
is worth a hundred schoolmasters."*
**George Herbert**

## MORALS

ᕗᕉ

**One of the most trying tasks** of many mothers is the teaching of morals to children, *especially* to boys.

This art or science has not yet been mastered even by the wisest, though some are more skilful in it than others. The best method so far as is known is by example rather than precept. It very frequently happens that those children who have had the most precepts thrust upon them in an inopportune manner turn out the worst.

The house where beauty, order, love, thoughtfulness of the rights of others, neatness, simplicity, and the daily doing of duty without parade and without complaint prevail; where rudeness, untruthfulness, and hypocrisy are hated and despised, does more to instil into the mind of the child good principles, than can be done in any other way. This is not the work of the mother alone, but of the father also.

### GOVERNESS

ༀ

**If a governess is to be employed**, parents can not use too much discrimination in choosing the lady to whom they are to trust the tuition of their little ones.

Economy should not be placed before all other considerations. Some people would pay their cook £25 a year without a qualm and yet grudge the same amount for a governess.

The day of the harsh unsympathetic disciplinarian is passed. A bright young girl who is fond of children is infinitely preferable to an elderly spinster whom age and care will probably have hardened and who often has but little sympathy with or understanding of youth.

Children and servants should be taught to look on the governess with respect.

### POCKET-MONEY

**A too liberal allowance of pocket-money** should never be made.

*There is nothing more conducive to extravagance in later years than an unlimited supply of pocket-money during childhood.*

The exact sum given must of course depend on circumstances. For children of from seven to ten years of age, 2d. to 3d. per week represents a good average. At a boarding-school the allowance of pocket-money should depend upon the prevailing regime. A parent should make a point of obtaining enlightenment in regard to this from the head master or mistress, regulating the allowance accordingly. Boys or girls at school should neither have more nor less pocket-money than that received by their companions.

## *Advice for good manners*

Grown-up people should also be very careful in
regard to their conversation before children.
Many things heard from their elders are stored up
in the small memories, and are apt to come out
upon the most awkward occasions.
Never indulge in scandal or gossip of any kind
before a child. Many parents err most flagrantly in
this respect, heedless of the fact that by so doing
they are sowing the seeds of unkindness and ill-
nature in the ears and minds of the little ones.

## SPEECH

**Good manners in speech** are most important. Children must make a habit of speaking slowly, and pronouncing words properly. They should never curse, or swear, or use vulgar words.

***A mother should not allow her children to be too much in the company of servants; and, what is very important, she should be particular to choose a nurse who speaks the King's English correctly, as a bad accent or Cockneyism is very soon acquired by the little ones, and exceedingly difficult to cure.***

The following words are very vulgar and should not be used; *'Faith I did' 'Faix I didn't' - Verrah, Wisha, Iyeh, Bedad, Whisht.*

The following sentences, besides being vulgar, are bad grammar:

*'She is going on to me'* instead of 'She is scolding me'

*'Rise the window'* instead of 'Raise the window'

*'I has'* instead of 'I have'

*'She do'* instead of 'She does'

*'She learned me my lesson'* instead of 'She taught me my lesson'

*'I done my sum'* instead of 'I did my sum'

*'I seen her yesterday'* should be 'I saw her yesterday'

– and many others which are constantly used, which teachers can correct when they notice them.

45

The following words are very often badly pronounced and should be corrected:

*Whin* for When
*Thim* for Them
*Agin* for Again
*Hin* for Hen
*Tay* for Tea
*Buy* for Boy
*Ketch the hin* for Catch the hen
*Tree* for Three
*Wit* for With
*Dis and dat* for This and that
*Writin* for Writing
*Singin* for Singing etc.
Also,
*I gave um* for I gave them
*Gim me* for Give me

- and many others which will be easily noticed and corrected.

## *Advice for good manners*

Always pronounce words properly; speak distinctly
but not too loud; a too loud voice is always the
sign of a very bad mannered child.

Do not clip words, always pronounce 'ing'
properly and correct any bad habits already
formed. Never say *'pratees'* for 'potatoes' and
never call potatoes *'spuds'*.

Do not think because older people say such things
they are correct, remember that they have not had
the advantages enjoyed by you, therefore excuses
should be made.

## SELF-CONSCIOUSNESS

❦

**E**very effort should be made to banish self-consciousness, which is after all but a deceitful form of vanity.

She who never thinks about herself at all will be sure to possess the charm of simplicity and nature in her manner.

Affectation and shyness are the two enemies of grace and must be overcome. But even then, a little attention to movements and tone of voice, as well as a knowledge of the ordinary forms of society are necessary.

Walk lightly, *glide along*; move things gently. Let all your movements be deliberate, but not *too* slow.

***Take sufficient time to do everything easily; hurry is always awkward.***

Let your movements be rounded, soft, and self-possessed - not angular, loud and hasty.

## *Advice for good manners*

The simpler the life led by children, the happier
they will be. Simple meals, regular hours, and
plenty of healthful exercise should be the keynote
of the regime of both nursery and
school-room. How pleasant it is to see the
enjoyment manifested by children so brought up
at the most simple treats and pleasures. They are
real children in every sense of the word, and in
later life they will have none but happy
recollections of a childhood passed in this way.

## KINDNESS

**Children should be watchful** and learn to render slight services to those around them. Give a footstool or book, if you see it is required, unasked - and be ready to show any graceful attention to those who are your elders or superiors.

It is in trifles we please most surely. No time is wasted which is spent in doing good; these are golden moments which you give to teaching a little sister, to helping your mother, to amusing her visitors.

## A WORD TO PARENTS

The lessons of obedience and self-control are ones a child should be made to learn early. This requires the utmost patience on the part of the mother. She must make it quite clear from the first that when she expresses a wish it must be obeyed, and never waver from her attitude of gentle firmness.

A child very soon learns if its parent's word is law, or if he can make her alter her mind by means of a little coaxing. It is very hard at times for a mother to resist the pretty childish graces which are often put forward as an inducement for her to waver from some precept or excuse some fault. However, once she gives way to such blandishments, she may give up all idea of ever having her children under perfect control.

*The knowledge that when mother says a thing she means it does more than anything else to win the respect and confidence of the little ones.*

## A WORD TO TEACHERS

∽

**A**nd now a word to teachers. Never keep children in school after school hours. It is equally hard on teacher and pupil, and it deprives the latter of necessary rest and recreation.

In the middle of the day allow the children to go to their dinners, for by keeping them late it means that they must bolt their food in order to be back at school in time.

Hurried meals are not good for either young or old, as they will in time cause indigestion and a host of stomach troubles.

*Teaching should be made a pleasure and not, as it so often is, a task for children.*

There are two ways in vogue of training children, and a third way of letting them grow up without any training whatever.

The two ways are training by precept and training by example. The former is good, the latter is better, but the best is a combination of both methods. Training by precept is, of course, far better than no training at all, but the reason it usually fails is that children generally do just as mother does – or father, too, for that matter.

When this is accomplished – even though it be a work of time – the home will be a happy and blessed one, and the children will benefit in later life by such counsel and guidance.

*The father or mother who is satisfied with giving children good food, good clothing, and good sleeping accommodation can scarcely be regarded as a good father or a wise mother.*

## MORAL MAXIMS

The most important things are purity of heart and correctness of principle. Intellect, wealth and beauty are of little value compared with goodness and, unless these gifts are accompanied with it, they serve to make their possessor unhappy within him or herself and disliked by her companions. Little ones can have good principles as well as grown people; the rules for forming them are few and simple.

~

Perhaps you have in your class a little girl who has not been at school as much as yourself; and because she cannot learn her lessons very readily, you laugh at her and call her stupid. Were you in her place, should you like to be so treated? If your heart answers 'No' you may be sure your conduct has been wrong.

~

Have you never caused your elder sisters a great deal of trouble by your carelessness or obstinacy?

## MORAL MAXIMS

Deal frankly with all, particularly with your parents or guardian. Never attempt to conceal your actions or motives. If you have broken or injured anything, go at once and avow it; and if you have been to blame in your dealings with companions, do not let silly pride or false shame prevent you from acknowledging it.

~

When you have formed a good resolution, never put off the time for carrying it into action. Every time a bad habit is indulged, it grows stronger, and is more difficult to overcome.

~

Always be attentive, respectful and affectionate to your parents.

~

Cherish love for your brothers and sisters.

*Never forget the Golden Rule.*
*To do unto others as you would have*
*others do to you.*

B.Y. 14. Dress Knicker Suit, in Black Velvet. Silk Facings, from 69/6 White Piqué Vests, 5/6

B.Y. 16. Tunic Suits for ages 3 to 6 years, in Cream or Navy Art Serges from 13/6 to 36/-. In Black or Navy Velveteen from 25/6. In "Liberty" art shades, from 21/6. In Cream Silk, 25/6 to 39/6. Silk Collars, 2/11, 3/6, 3/11 each.

B.Y. 17. Dinner Suit in Black Dress Suiting, in quality size, to 11 years, 47/6, rise full size, and quality, size to 14 years, 5/6, rise 1/6 size. Jackets and ties only, 27/6, rise full size, quality, 41/-, rise 1/6. Black Dress Trousers, 8/11 to 15/6. White Piqué Waistcoats, from 5/6.

B.Y. 20. Drummer Gowns for boys 3 to 7 years. In quality from 10/6, latest quality, 15/6 to 21/6.

B.Y. 21. Jersey Suit in white, navy, myrtle, cardinal, brown, sky, etc., 6/6; Cap 1/- extra. "Two Smacks" Sound Collar, 6/6 first size, better quality, 6/6 to 12/6

B.Y. 23. The "Kensington" Suit, in Black Velveteen, 27/- to 35/6. In Black or Navy Cloth, 30/6 to 37/6. White Piqué Waistcoats, from 6/6

B.Y. 13. Double-breasted Motor Coats, in warm fleece or Nap Cloths. Lined Wool, 33/6 to 63/-. Lined Leather, 83/- to 105/-.

B.Y. 20. Young Gentleman's Umbrellas, newest Handles, strong frames and reliable covers. 8/6, 8/11, 10/6, 13/6

B.Y. 51. Young Gentleman's Walking Sticks, choice selection, from 3/6 to 9/6

B.Y. 13. Young Gentleman's Dressing Gown, in lawn or grey imitation Camel-hair, very soft and warm, 18/6 to 27/6, according to size. In Navy Frieze, 13/6 to 27/-. In pure Camel-hair natural or navy, 33/6 to 33/-.

B.Y. 46.

B.Y. 51. Young Gentleman's Socks, in Black or Tan Cashmere, Harrods' complete School class for Sports for 8/6. In extra fine quality, 1/11 pair. In Black Cashmere, extra strong quality, 1/3, 1/11, 2/6 pair. In Sport Silk, latticework finish, 3/6 pair.

B.Y. 11. Eton Jacket and Waistcoat, 18/6 to 30/6. Trousers, Grey Hairline, from 8/11 to 12/6. Fancy Stripe, from 10/6 to 21/6. Silk Hats, 10/6, 13/6, 18/6.

B.Y. 33. Covert Coat to fit boys 5 to 11 years, 15/6 to 42/-, according to size and march. 9/11. Riding Breeches, in Whipcord or Buckskin serge cd, 23/6 to 9/6. In Strong Tweeds, Buckskin wrapseat, from 15/6. In Strong Tweeds without wrapping, from 6/6.

B.Y. 31. Young Gentleman's Gloves, Strong Tan Cape, 3/6, 3/11 pair. Tan or Grey Nacks, 3/9 pair. Tan Doeskin, lined wool, for wrist, 2/11 pair Tan Doeskin, lined wool, 5/-, 5/6 pair. Fur Gloves, 6/6 pair. Wool Gloves in white, heather, or grey, 1/6, 1/11 pair.

B.Y. 37. Rugby Suit to fit boys 5 to 13 years. In Tweeds from 18/- to 48/-. In Navy Serges, 25/6 to 48/-.

B.Y. 18. S.B. Yearly Overcoat, in dark grey Cheviot 21/6 to 30/6. Fancy Tweed, 23/6 to 30/6. Navy Beaverar Nap, 21/6 to 63/-.

11

# "Woman's Own" Dress Chat

## THE YOUNG GIRL'S ATTIRE

The little daughter has not sufficient clothes until a costume, coat-dress and a simple frock appear in her wardrobe, for she can find a use for them all—no matter how rich, how poor she may be! More than one idea is shown here for the mother to copy for her.

22,170

22,171

22,173

22,175

22,174

CHILDREN'S clothes nowadays seem to be planned deliberately to imitate those intended for their elders until the young people become walking fashion sketches, or cut unusual and striking figures that Nature never intended them to.

Looking at the young people belonging to well-to-do sections of the community, this fact is everyday more and more evident. It is, therefore, a happy relief when one travels inland, midst the rural district, and sees the little ones trotting off to school or to church on a Sunday dressed in the simplest pinafore dress, the plainest coat and skirt.

When dress is being dealt with in a paper, however, mothers look for the unusual, the " new " creations. They are already familiar with what their children and they themselves wore years ago. No matter what position a woman is in, she likes to make her children's things a little bit in the fashion, and so the happy medium in dress has been chosen, and such designs are illustrated here.

A girl may be considered well supplied with clothes if she has a good coat, a costume, and a dress or dresses in addition to the essential undergarments, stockings, and shoes. She can even go hatless, and still be dressed.

The young girls have been given the cost-dress, an invention for mothers and grown-up sisters, but nevertheless, she—between the age of eight and fourteen—can look well in this type of garment; and the little maidens have been heard to vote for the coat-dress in preference to a costume. "One thing to put on instead of two, mother," was the reason given by a little maid of twelve. It is therefore a good idea to make one of these walking dresses, and try the experiment, as it can always be used as a school-dress in the winter.

Like the grown woman, the little maid sometimes looks much better in the all-in-one garment, while others are at their best in a plain blouse and skirt or short, full coat.

Dresses intended to be made in washing material are very plain but prettily cut this year. There are two styles shown here which would suit almost any child. No. 22,170 is made to put on altogether, and so is the other, No. 22,174, although it would be just as pretty if the skirt were detachable in this.

Tussore and linen, piqué and drill are amongst the most popular materials chosen for making the children's things, because of their durability. There is no lining needed, so the slightly higher price for these materials is allowed for; and it is more satisfactory to work upon really substantial materials than cheap stuff that will not wear well.

**THE ETIQUETTE COLLECTION** *Collect the set!*
**ETIQUETTE FOR COFFEE LOVERS**
Fresh coffee - the best welcome in the world!
Enjoy the story of coffee drinking,
coffee etiquette and recipes.

**ETIQUETTE FOR CHOCOLATE LOVERS**
Temptation through the years.
A special treat for all Chocolate Lovers.

**THE ETIQUETTE OF NAMING THE BABY**
*'A good name keeps its lustre in the dark.'*
Old English Proverb

**THE ETIQUETTE OF AN ENGLISH TEA**
How to serve a perfect English afternoon tea;
traditions, superstitions, recipes and how to read your
fortune in the tea-leaves afterwards.

**THE ETIQUETTE OF ENGLISH PUDDINGS**
Traditional recipes for good old-fashioned
puddings - together with etiquette notes
for serving.

**ETIQUETTE FOR GENTLEMEN**
*'If you have occasion to use your handkerchief
do so as noiselessly as possible.'*

*Copper Beech Gift Books
are designed and printed
in Great Britain*